Your House Is Floating

For Cindy —
With much love
and gratitude!

Your House Is Floating

Poems by

Susan Whitmore

Liquid Light Press

Premium Chapbook First Edition

ISBN-10: 0-9883072-2-7

ISBN-13: 978-0-9883072-2-3

Liquid Light Press

poetry that speaks to the heart

www.liquidlightpress.com

Cover Art by Robert Ronci
(*www.beatsbyesk.com*)

Cover Design by M. D. Friedman
(*www.mdfriedman.com*)

Photo of Poet by Willow Baum
(*www.smallplanetpartners.com*)

Contents

Cathedral

My room is sunny and clean:
A table, a chair, work I say I'm doing,
Fresh air through the window, tea on the stove,

My body sheathed in its fine envelope —
The whole package as white as the tablecloth.
You come, thinking this is my home,

So beautiful you ache when you must go.
What else would you think?
This is what I show you. But

The cathedral's stone walls sweat
On the inside, moldy with supplication
And the fierce stare of gargoyles,

The high, dark ceilings I cannot fathom.
My body is nothing in there,
A piece of heat fallen from the candle,

Black wax frozen into a splatter.
The Virgin goes on with her entreaties:
Give it up, my sweet. Throw the doors wide.

Ice

Black ice and the brakes don't matter.
The heater never did start heating
And it's cold baby, cold in the car.
I thought I knew where I was going

Only now it won't stop——I did it,
I did it after all even though I thought
I would not and was driving straight.
I spoke my crush on you. The skid is on.

Tent

At midnight I put my Circe on your Phiona.

The kerosene lantern burned an orange orb
On the green skin of the sweating tent
Where we lay in cotton sleeping bags
In the days before down and polyfiber.

The air outside was thick with fireflies
And dumb June bugs that whirr, whirred
In our swimming pool-stained hair
Gleaming stiff and shiny, chlorine tangle.

My belly was heavy and jittery with possibility:
Blood yet to come and red wine not yet drunk
In the la la land of adult love.
We were both awake and not blinking,

Our index, ring and pinkie fingers twined
And thigh-to-thigh, taut as high-wire gymnasts
In a sparkling rage of crimson fire sequins
As we stepped out carefully on the girl-line.

Forsythia

At thirteen, the black-boot, square-toed boy
Came calling, riding his moped
Fourteen miles for my French kiss
In a glen below my parents' home,

Green with lilies about to burst
Into bloom. The woods' cool dark
Kept pace with light dappled
Through the poplar ceiling:

New spring leaves, muddy ground
And my fingers on his trembling.

I'm still surprised by any wet,
Luscious thing — the flavor of dew,
Sweet spit on a tongue pointed firmly
Toward the body's craving.

The dance of senses, hand in hand
With nature, began here: First
In waiting for the sound of the motor
On the street, my ears keening;

Then the short walk through brush

And new forsythia, down a damp bank

To the shaded bedroom of

Flowers yet to be, for fifteen kisses, exactly.

Fluid

This is juicy: Despite despair,
The muscular heart goes on beating —
A ventricled bit of meat betting on

Its bid with the celestials, who said:
Sing! Sing until you can't.
The aorta sends music downward

And upward and sideways into
The larger body, that the limbs might
Break into rhythm and harmony,

Sinews and tendons stretched across
The corporal lyre, the body's instrument
Now lively and thrumming with joy.

What course does blood have but hope?
Love threads its way into every sweet organ —
The fantastic lungs, stable stomach,

Melancholy bowels and the bright brain,
The electric spine now informing
The whole skeleton's elegant bones.

Sunset

On Highway 435 into Kansas my hands are careful
On the wheel, the muscles of my heart vigilant
Around the veins they squeeze — four chambers of beat
And a whole body to keep going. I'm thinking earth

And country people more intact and at ease than I,
The gentle cheek's acceptance of wind, mind no obstacle
To time or how much time it takes to travel ten miles
Going seventy. Early evening and light is late. I imagine

Heavy cows moan now for milking, beady-eyed crows
Settling in the poplars, nutty oats poured before horses.
The creak of iron, stable doors bolted against the cold.
The man who proffers oats feels horse body come to rest,

Heat rising with each breath, warmth inside wooden walls.
The woman who wed the man rests her brow against
The carpet of a cow's side, her palms and fingers easing
Steaming milk into a bucket. And I am among the crazies

Going as fast as we can without dying or getting a ticket.
Still, I have my own boon: The magenta sunset spreads
A florid skirt against sky, revealing her secret —
A blood-red opening and fuchsia thighs she dares me kiss.

Snowman

After Tim Seibles

Avalanche of avant-garde in my bedroom:

Peony-scent, unseasonably tepid rain,

Traffic splash on the street, water running

In gutters. It's February — an impossible time

For peonies, or these ripe lemons now,

On electric air through the window.

All the household plants and I, pricking

Up our skin. A snowman lover drops

Bits of himself under my embrace.

The smooth, white face fades, stick arms

Drop off, black belt and bowler hat

Talismans floating on a pool of water.

The puddle that was lover extinguishes me

On scent of lemons and peonies, thunder's

Thick sound and the rain, a strident torrent

Demanding earth's suck. The snowman

Has no constitution, and I am a knot of bones

Rising to the surface where water meets air.

Secure and bright, the stars look down and laugh.

Filigree glitter on water, a mosaic of glee.

Consummation complete: No matter, no one lives

To tell the tale. Who needs a mouth or tongue

When the whole body has become kiss,

The whole body dissolved into wonder?

Ice Cream

Valentine's Day

You sweet milk gone good sugar

Our lips meet soft snap stop

Dollop *Oh don't do that* chocolate-

Thing vanilla cherry pringle

My principal place is tingling

Jimmies on mine yours hot sauce

I want all of it cream and curve

And your thighs *May I please*

First you said *No* I said *No* nuts

Cookie dough is so passé *Let's go*

Yes with yogurt swirl lo-fat so fine

I'm right here honey waiting for mine

Moth

I.

You are a moth in my mouth
Quiet frail fluttering
So delicate and I do not want
To hurt the fragile wing

You are a precious point
When I am with you
I cannot breathe or see
Anything but shimmering

And now you are gone
To New York City where
Your fine hips hold forth
On sidewalks and sofas

Of exquisite places I am not
But I am glad for you because
You are bigger than Kansas City
Or New York, just you being

II.

I am a cup with a crack
In its porcelain bottom
I want to hold everything lucent
And wet but the cup leaks

I know now there is nothing
Other than this open place in me
Where you have come home
A precious point glimmering

Fingernail moon upside down
This while we have been here
And there before, New York
Kansas City it does not matter

I have held you down
On my own green couch
And let you go back and forth
A moth in my mouth flying out

Rice

You say you'd climb a mountain,
That you've ascended already
With walking stick and begging bowl:

Calluses thick on your soles,
The red burn on your cheeks more flame
Than you'd imagined. Muscles

Grown taut as wood in your calves
And thighs have made you a new man,
A man who doesn't need me:

The journey is enough — salt
Creased into the crevices of your face,
Knees finally bent low on the stone

Before an altar of another divinity.
Now I'm a brown sparrow
Alighting on the temple roof

Built of wind-blown sticks
Fragrant with incense, beak open
For one grain of rice from your bowl.

Boat

I would like not minding, whatever travels my heart.

— Jane Hirshfield, *Metempsychosis*

Darling, I know it is not your love

Which makes me free or your distance a prison.

The still eye at the hurricane's center

Is the only spot inside emotion entirely

Disconnected and unmoved by anything —

Pine planks from the dock, white sails loosened

From their rigging, a skipper's hat, feathers

From the herring gull. And here we are now

In stormy seas. Here I am in the boat that keeps

Sinking, this boat I keep patching with hope

And prayer. One would think despair a good teacher —

But no, I only come to love the boat more each time

It sinks under the weight of feeling. And no,

It's not love, but that sickness, an attachment

To too much sugar or salt: One makes me fat,

The other, too thin. Obesity and emaciation.

So no, it's not love, but a boat sickness.

Constellation

Orion strings his star-studded belt across the sky's hip:
Any warrior knows it's unwise to sleep without a weapon
Nearby. The street is silent but for one dog, that rake,

Howling two blocks over at Venus in heat, all heaven
Waiting for his owner to come home. I'm dreaming
My husband, how he paced the halls at night the summer

I slept pregnant with the prospect we both feared,
Painting fevered pictures of roads ascending horizon
Through fields thick with poppies, tiger lilies pointing

Their tongues at the Seven Sisters clustered against
The blow, Big Dipper turned upward and back to catch
The glittering afterbirth. All stars shine beyond the burn

Long gone out, an echo so real there's no salvation
But to believe in the future, the firmament projected
Back of the eye — a mother and father, a child yet to be.

Dreck and Music

It's the memory of how I loved him:
The forever-promise giving way to another need
As the furniture trembled and the hallways narrowed,
The electric wires behind drywall tangling like hair
And humming betrayal. Everything changes.

It's the memory of how I loved him,
And how I love him still only more finely
Now I don't need him, what rises above the dreck
Of the broken home — the cracked crystal,
A thermometer's mercury running loose in the sink

And freed of fever, an asbestos cloud released
After years from its wallpaper layers,
A door swung open evermore. The real promise
Shines now in sunlight between the strands of our child's hair —
How gentle the white scalp, the sweet skull just beneath.

Tower

Surely anger has its own love and bedfellow.

Why else would you climb the winding stair

Again and again, exhausting yourself

Completely as when you would stay awake for days

Soiling the sheets with a new desire?

Rage has its way.

Ringlets fall in perfect circles from your head.

Porcelain and austere as Isolde, you wait

In the tower of your own construct

As certain and nebulous as the idea of God.

On high, the view is fine.

You can see an enemy approaching miles ahead of time.

But your ringlets grow into tangles

And no hand reaches you there.

Isolation your sex, solitude your food.

Lock

Tonight love shares itself with hate.

You exist next to yourself, cannot

Rise above the fact of your own back

Turned to your touch in bed——

The sheets cold and angry with sweat

And fear, the need to push despondency out.

You are the exploding girl

Who splits herself widely into nothing.

Intimacy is a wind that blows, or doesn't.

There's nobody to hold on to

Though you lay hands constantly

On yourself——sinew, tendon, skin——

Thinking this vessel holds everything,

Seeing this self as a key.

But you are not a key

And the locks remain fast against you.

Sex is not an answer.

Lie down and sleep when you can.

When you can't, wake too early

In still dark, watch city lights blinking

Beyond slits in the shade.

You are far off from the city

And the city lights are like knives

Brailing your body, an echo of what.

Why can't you touch yourself kindly?

I do place blame:

I am asking you to change.

Stone

I'm no prophet, but I can tell
When blood falls too quickly,
I can tell when the entrails are tangled
Into unnatural knots on the stone:
Their pattern spells yearning,
That hard gallop toward God
In entirely the wrong direction.

How can I do this without words?
Someone has to mention that
The intestines are the wrong color,
The liver twice the size it should be,
Black blood running northward in a rush
To the brain, instead of gently
In the four directions, from the heart.

I'll admit it. There are times when
I want the one I love to lift me
Like a child from the stone, put the puzzle
Of my guts together and name me whole.
The one I love will love me broken:
I will not wake up one day suddenly one piece,
Having run together like mercury.

It's me splayed wide on the gray stone

Of my life, split from my mouth to my sex—

It's for me alone to look inside and listen.

There's a singing and a crying both

I cannot decipher, a code

Composed in its own language:

Of the body, not of words.

Eurydice

Your white hand, Eurydice, rises from the bath
Until water slides down to reveal the fine lines
Of your fingers and a pristine pool in your palm.

Just so, you wish your beloved reaching through
Cumulus billowing above the earth roof
Of the house, sweeping clouds away to bare

One spot of surprising blue, drop the sun down
To embrace and lift, carry you up and through.
Some lovers cry before the other is gone.

Your union was replete with grief even while
You lived and rolled in moonlit flowers with him,
Lilac and hyacinth honey, nectar beneath your back.

You recall tears falling hot as daylight on your brow
At night after his long leaning over you was over,
Your breath slowed into sobs, the arc of a love song.

Now your days are unending hours in the bath,
Mouth shut tight and head submerged, hair swirling
Like seaweed in the swift current of the underworld.

Ghosts

The brain is wider than the sky.

— Emily Dickinson

Most ghosts you don't personally know.

There was the malevolent one
Who blanketed you with despair
When you lay in bed with your first lover,
Just so you'd hold each other close.

There was the benevolent one
Who sang with a choir of children
Just as you entered the twilight of sleep
The summer you stayed in Spain.

And the naked one who raged
In your backyard pond, drowning,
While the ghost with a perfect profile
Stole your clogs from the front porch
The night before the daffodils opened.

But every dawn, it's your mother
Hovering gray above your dresser
And drawing your silver-backed brush
Through the strands of her auburn hair.

Frame and Figure

I.

The Nude is held intact by its frame:

Black tree trunk cured beyond existence,

Sap no longer lively, existing now

To embrace a woman's intricate space.

Four limbs stretched to four corners —

Hand and foot and hand and foot —

Body exposed pink and gray, a bit of blue

Around skin's edges where the outer

World kisses the inner membrane,

Angels whispering to ready veins,

Keep on living — even as devils raise hair

Back of neck and scalp, voicing doubt.

II.

I have a home, two children

And work I do to keep things intact —

Food in the mouth, ink in the pen,

Sandalwood incense on the altar.

Each night, four limbs to four corners:

Bare belly exposed to the angels'

Precursor answer to incessant questions

While those devils confound every deed.

Each day, I find myself on my knees.

The perfect figure will crumble at death.

Meanwhile: the luminous and spread torso.

A blatant body bounded by frame.

Paper

I.

Almost origami, a crisp-white

Orchid with a crimson dangling tongue

Grows out of the moss stump.

II.

I filled the bathtub with paper:

Bills, yellow post-it notes that had lost their stick,

To-do lists, all my business cards.

III.

A thin girl in an emerald dress

Came to me in a dream and said——

Don't you know? It's time.

Your House Is Floating

I.

The strata of body signify spirit: skin, flesh, bone, center.

Somewhere outside body is the larger body,

Galaxy floating and rooted in gravity's pull, both aerial and earth.

You are buried and released here as well as there — in element and space.

The universe turns, is transformed.

That you were once a child is evident in your face.

II.

Mount Rushmore floats on magma. Nebraska's wheat fields float like

ponds.

Arctic icebergs float too, of course. Your house is floating.

Skin floats above the bone on a current of blood and marrow.

Grass is filled with liquid sun. Your breath is floating.

And that love you lost floats, muscular, in the sinew's ribbon

And tendon's string — singing what does not float, but flies.

III.

On Venus volcanoes leak lava like milk from a mother's breast:

The planet is alive and flourishing.

And on Earth embryos float in the womb,

Turned in salty fluid toward Polaris and the moon.

Your feet are planted most often in dirt; your head, in air.

When sleeping, you are what the fair universe floats on.

About the Author

An East Coast transplant to the Kansas City area, Susan Whitmore's aesthetic melds bovine beauty with the beat of the jazz greats. Previous books include *The Melinda Poems* (Pudding House Press 2004), *The Sacrifices* (Mellen Poetry Press 1992) and *The Invisible Woman* (Singular Speech Press 1991). With a degree in ancient Greek from Vassar College and a Master of Fine Arts from Emerson College, she taught creative writing and literature at the University of Nebraska-Lincoln and the University of Missouri-Kansas City and was executive director of The Writers Place, a nonprofit literary arts center in Kansas City. Since 2010 she has been a vice president at First Call, an agency serving individuals and families impacted by substance use disorders. Her work has appeared in *CrossCurrents, Dalhousie Review, Georgia Review, Georgetown Review, I-70 Review, Melusine, New Letters* and *Poet Lore*, among others.

Credits and Acknowledgements

Poems in this manuscript previously appeared in the following publications:

"Eurydice"—*Melusine*, Washington, District of Columbia, 2012

"Frame and Figure"—*I-70 Review*, Kansas City, Missouri, 2011

"Snowman"—*Poet Lore*, Bethesda, Maryland, 2011

"Stone"—*I-70 Review*, Kansas City, Missouri, 2011

"Sunset"—*I-70 Review*, Kansas City, Missouri, 2011

OTHER BOOKS BY SUSAN WHITMORE

The Invisible Woman (Singular Speech Press 1991)

The Sacrifices (Mellen Poetry Press 1992)

The Melinda Poems (Pudding House Press 2004)

Other Books from Liquid Light Press (All Liquid Light Press books are available directly from *www.liquidlightpress.com* or from any of the current major global distribution channels including Amazon, Barnes and Noble, the iBookstore and the Ingram Catalog)

Leaning Toward Whole, Poems by M. D. Friedman (Released June, 2011)

This poetry chapbook from the international award winning poet, M. D. Friedman, contains pieces both poignant and personal. *Leaning Toward Whole* speaks to both the universal and the everyday, both the moment and the millennium.

The Miracle Already Happening - Everyday Life with Rumi, Poems by Rosemerry Wahtola Trommer (Released December, 2011)

Rosemerry Wahtola Trommer's superb collection of poems, inspired by Rumi, is full of heart, humor, peace and wisdom. This chapbook gracefully flings us from our routine into the joy of life, bristles with surprise and dances with mystic vision.

Spiral, Poems by Lynda La Rocca (Released March, 2012)

Award winning poet, Lynda La Rocca, creates a compelling poetic and melodic discourse from the persistent cravings and fears inside of each of us. This book is both as darkly sweet and satisfying as chocolate and as nourishing and healing as mother's chicken soup.

From the Ashes, Poems by Wayne A. Gilbert (Released June , 2012)

Master jazz Sufi poet, Wayne A. Gilbert, chronicles the loss of his mother with powerful, bittersweet honesty to create this beautiful collection of poems that is universal in its scope, transcendent in the depth of its understanding and exquisitely musical in form.

ah, Poems by Rachel Kellum (Released July, 2012)

Rachel Kellum's first published book is a transparent poetic odyssey into the ethereal that is both provocative and inspirational. In *ah* Rachel Kellum demonstrates a maturity of craft that bespeaks the power of poetry to suggest what logic always struggles to explain about our divine nature.

Catalyst, Poems by Jeremy Martin (Released December, 2012)

This is Jeremy Martin's first book of poetry and is a mind field of delight. It explodes with incendiary insight, cosmic playfulness and dizzying joy. It lifts us up on the back of a rocket and leaves in the weightless orbit of inner self.

Of Eyes and Iris by Erika Moss Gordon (Released March, 2013)

Erica Moss Gordon's first book of poetry shines with the purity of a mountain stream, dances with sunlight, and shivers with the chill of perception. Refreshing with its simplicity yet rich in wisdom, her poetry punctuates its quite voice with echoes of illumination.